Wet Matches

Taryn Miller

Presentation by *BookLeaf Publishing*

Web: www.bookleafpub.com

E-mail: info@bookleafpub.com

ISBN: 9789357619950

First edition 2022

DEDICATION

For my husband, Tyler, who continues to show up for me every day. I wouldn't want to know what life looks like without you. Thank you. I love you.

ACKNOWLEDGEMENT

My father, Jamie, who always traded poems with me via text, recited poetry to me at random and encouraged me to write ever since I was a child.

To my daughters, my inspiration, my motivation, my everything.

To my lifelong and steadfast friend, Jarett, who read almost all of these poems before they ever saw paper. Thank you for being my sounding board in life, death, love and art.

And finally, to Dorothy Parker, whose poetry has permanently changed the way I perceive the world.

PREFACE

Do not ever be afraid to say what you feel, either in person or on paper. If you can find the right words and arrange them just so, you may learn a lot more about yourself.

Change of Seasons

Drops of dew
Silvery blue,
Nestled on the blades.
That grow in sun
Where bare feet run,
Where memories are made.
I see them from behind the glass,
While tucked away inside.
Sensing Autumns on the cusp,
And Mother Nature lied.

Medium

Fools will say love conquers all
And writers will fawn and cheer,
If you've ever known how it is to fall
You'd beg to differ here.
Love is but a piece of art
Messy and incomplete,
You have high hopes from the start
Your brush strokes on repeat.
But love will only conquer you
Your heart, your mind, your soul,
It'll even trick your body too
When you're down the rabbit hole.
Love, it doesn't conquer all
It terrorizes more,
And when it tears you limb from limb
You'll beg to know what for.
Perhaps you'll try to stop it
Lay chains around your heart,
Eventually, you will submit
And that itself, is art.

Yearning

3

Woven are the branches
Undisturbed
Agonizingly tangled
Immensely perturbed
Casting a shadow
Over vicious terrain
Perpetuating darkness
Encouraging pain
Twice calls a cardinal
From somewhere above
To seek out the crow
And prophesy love
Silky blue-black
It takes flight through the trees
For sought after sunlight
Fresh air and seas
The foliage, dense
Creates such a thicket
The crow descends back to moss
Isn't life wicked?

The Keeper

If I could name a shooting star
And pull it from the sky,
I'd grasp it tightly in my fist
And refuse to let it fly.
I'd keep it at my bedside
Fall asleep amidst the glow,
And hear it tap inside a jar
With nowhere left to go.
I'd quizzically observe it
As it races all about,
Then deem it fine to call it mine
And never let it out.

A Girl Named Sonny

5

What say you have a trillium
Stark white with petals three,
You plant it in the garden
Underneath the linden tree.
There it grows for years and years
A joy to watch it bloom,
It withers down as seasons pass
And colder temperatures loom.
Then one day it's brought to you
It's long stem torn in half,
By a tiny girl with ginger curls
And a wicked little laugh.
Despite how much you love her
You can't help but feel sad,
But in the tiny mind of tiny girl
She gave you all she had.

Hypocrisy

A man can take a lady home
Or two or ten or twenty,
But lest a lady lay with one
By default, she's had many.

Fiend

7

Sleep is hard to come by,
And waking is so hard,
I'd like to dream a happy dream,
Then I'll let down my guard.
But when my eyes are closing,
And I see what lies beneath,
My sleeping mind is wicked,
And waking; sweet relief.

Fervent

When the moon is glowing,
And words dance on your tongue.
When your skin's like radio static,
And your body comes undone.
When you're yearning for the moment,
When there's nothing left to say.
Your mind has left the building,
And the whole world melts away.
When he looks at you through narrowed eyes
And you lick your eager lips,
Remember that he's but a man,
Then try to come to grips!

Back To Blue

9

Your mind was an enigma
And your body in disrepair,
I hadn't seen you lately
But I felt you everywhere.
My thoughts consumed with worry
As you traveled overseas,
I kept all of your letters
But was never put at ease.
You called me at all hours
Shared secrets for me to keep,
Then you hid inside the woods
Where you slowly went to sleep.
It never seemed conceivable
Since I was unaware,
I haven't seen you lately
But I feel you everywhere.

Restraint

Torn in two
Between the choice,
Before you know
You've lost your voice,
Til someone
A question poses,
The door you opened
Somehow closes.

Fear of Heights

You are this!
I said to he.
No you are!
He said back to me.
And then he lashed
His sharpened tongue,
Listing all the wrong I'd done.
If you don't like it
You can go!
But that is when I came to know,
Of all the men under the Sun;
I'd chosen me the evil one.

Wet Matches

There are some things
Throughout our lives
That will always fail to please.

Birds may sing
And church bells ring
But other things will cease.

So to any storm
That comes our way
We'll batten down the hatches.

And live to love
Another day
And forget about wet matches.

Orca

If you try to see reason
You may come up with doubt.
If you follow rules blindly
You're better without.
If you say 'count me in'
To be one of the many,
You'll wait for the carrot
But there won't be any.
Should you dare to wake up
With a whistle to blow,
You'll be among the first to go.

Hindrance

Call a number
In a phone
Suggest that they
Should take you home
Reach for stars
But come up empty
Then call another
There are plenty
And when the list
At last runs out
You've planted your own
Seeds of doubt.

Surface Area

I've had an epiphany
And it has got the best of me,
While others live so flawlessly
I drown in a colossal sea.

Whenever something is amiss
I swear that I'm not made for this,
While others live in ignorant bliss
I'm plummeting down the abyss.

But if I were a fly upon their wall
Would I feel resentful or appalled?
Are they mere moments from a fall
Into oblivion, like me?

Olly Olly Oxen Free

I can still place the day I knew
That I'd been truly had.
He told me that he loved me
But I didn't say it back.

There was a time the world was mine
But I didn't trust a soul.
Then he waltzed into my life
And quickly made me whole.

I knew then that I too loved him
Much to my dismay.
Then on and on for years on years
I loved him more each day.

We went about the whole nine yards
Babies, vows and trials.
And even though some days were tough
I loved him all the while.

He's all my favorite parts of me
That I had been without.
And when he says he loves me now
I believe him without doubt.

He, The Beholder

If I could change my eyes and face
And cover myself in satin and lace
Then maybe I could find a place,
To fit the mold
And take up space.

I'd only have to curl my hair
Be sure to match my underwear
Have flawless skin that's soft and fair,
Apply makeup
That looks "barely there".

I wouldn't have much more to lose
If I donned a pair of six inch shoes
My legs would be a grown man's muse,
Then I'd surely be
The girl they'd choose.

I'll sit for dinner, yet I won't eat
To keep my body trim and neat
And when I think my job's complete,
They'll tell me still
I'm obsolete.

The Afterparty

Pray to promises
And place your faith,
They promise you
It's worth the wait.
'Cause when you get there
You will know,
Where all the loyal people go.
And those who chose
To not believe,
Are someplace else
You cannot see.

Rebirth

A single sapling
Beat the blade
That cut down its creator.
And grand it grows
Sat by the stump
That quickly crumbles later.
A highly hailed
Sign of success
From a fickle Mother Nature.
An aspirational
Feat of force
And life, and love, and labor.

Tango

A prompt
Which triggers self-belief,
Can work a thousand wonders.
An event
Which causes pain and grief,
Can cause a thousand blunders.

I Was Once

A child yearns to be fully grown
And make decisions of their own,
They count the days til they can drive
On open roads and feel alive.
Shortly after, they tempt a drink
This is the life; or so they think,
A job and home are next in line
And sure, at first this all seems fine.
Then they take a man or wife
And build themselves a decent life,
Raising children of their own
They fear the day they're fully grown.
Then who was once a child too
Discovers something so brand new,
They had it good but wished it away
Now they're yearning for more time to play.

www.ingramcontent.com/pod-product-compliance
Lightning Source LLC
LaVergne TN
LVHW021354200726
843509LV00014B/2851